Mercurial

Emanuel   Galimidi

Presentation by *BookLeaf Publishing*

Web: www.bookleafpub.com

E-mail: info@bookleafpub.com

ISBN: 9789360941314

First edition 2024

*To my son. No matter what you
love or what you do, know
that all you need is inside
of you.*

ACKNOWLEDGEMENT

My wife. She's the muse I'll never let lose.

PREFACE

The cool thing about art is that whether you keep it to yourself or share with the world, it doesn't change, only those who experience it do.

Love is the answer? Says who?

Why is love the answer?

When revenge tastes so sweet on
my lips…
When it cuts where you bleed
the most…
When that desire feels so
unquenchable…so, inevitable…
When the sadness is so
alluring…

Because love brings forth
light.
Because love is, light
Because light allows us to
choose between it and darkness.

In that cold room. Shut out
from the world, darkness offers
you no choice, only an empty
demand

And what are each of you, if
not free to choose.

And what are we if not the most
choice of all things

Choose the light

choose you.

To every loss I can't remember

To the memories I don't
remember anymore good and bad

Hiding in plain site
Hiding all the pain inside
When did you leave me?

I didn't notice until it was
too late.
Until you had crept out the
back door doing your best not
to disrupt my new dreams, my
new complaints, my newest
regret.

Rise

When you are cast into the
darkest of pits whether by the
hand of another or one more
familiar, your very own, rise.

As you lay there broken, torn
and listless, rise.

As you lay there resentful and
remorseful all at once, rise.

As you lay there less than
before then, rise.

Because when you do, you rise
with what is left of you which
is greater than what was once
all of you.

Pizza and Wine

A pizza pie was shared many
times
So much it seemed the planets
aligned
Our words and mouths
intertwined
All of that, so sublime
But then our time became,
just…. sometimes
Was it you or was it I
Who told this dream goodbye
No matter, we can always say it
was just the wine.

Our ticket

We only got one ride on this
roller coaster you and me.

Jumped in kinda late but
somehow right on time for that
beautiful summer time sky.

Wondering why there's only one
shot, one loop, one wild ride
for this vast romance.

No sense in looking back at
tracks or over your back
wonderin' bout this and that

Just watch as they all
disappear, as we ride over them
just you and I

Eyes forward
Arms tucked over your belly
holding onto our ticket
Our one first ticket
Our one last ticket

One ticket to never thinking
twice
One ticket you and I
Just have one in our hands
Hoping to God that we never
land

Promised Fate

Keeping a promise is divine. It is how we participate in authoring the future we want, and not one signed and sealed by fate alone.

Our heaven

What if there is no better
place.

What if it's just as wide and
deep, as pained and sweet as
this place right here.

Wouldn't that be something.

Wouldn't that be something to
pray for.

First Day

Trying to be a bystander but
feeling less than innocent.
Sitting wondering why all I
noticed was the replica watch I
didn't want anyway.
Trying to look busy with these
idle hands
You're no devil I know but for
me it's really too hard to
show.
Hard to show I am more than my
dead stare.
More alive than in disrepair
More than just the old scars
that open every time I walk out
that apartment door.
All I do is stare out,
wondering how long this will
take.
Knowing how good it will feel
to be free of this heaviness
draped over my shoulders
layered with words I still do
not know
Still wrapped in beliefs they
could not know

And yet on that first day we
started a show
A show that never ends
No curtain call my friends
Just an itch that follows me
around with no end.
So I leave like I do every
time.
Running to that freedom and
that bright sunshine
Back to the comfort of my home
where God knows me and I know
him.
And no discomfort is felt
again.

Stormbound

Doubt rips through my heart as
an ocean of worry washes over
my bow.

Each wave punishes my wayward
keel.

Eyes burn from an ocean of
tears.
Of a future I have reason to
fear.
Terror sweeps and tears at my
sails.
No safe harbor to be found.

Still afloat I inhale focus and
exhale the dread in my salty
lungs.

I grip the wheel and turn her
neither starboard nor port but
stormbound as far and as deep
as those gales howl.

All at once I am swallowed
whole.

The wind and my sails are now
indistinguishable.

The deck, the ocean floor.
The sea and joined as one.
We look out and chart our
course.
His gaze was unmistakable.

The brother you know

What if two brothers tangle and
Abel killed Cain?

What if the best in you does
the worst?

What does the best of you
become when there's nothing to
aspire to?

Seems best we lost Abel to
forever gain Cain.

Who are you exactly?

You always wanted to be is the worst thing you can say to me, because that means I am not who I was meant to be.

The Perfect Crime

The crime wasn't stealing my heart, it was returning it to me without a scratch.

Much to do about nothing.

So I pontificate not because
I'm the only or the better but
because I don't mind the doing.
Because thinking about things
is how you get to understand
those things people don't want
to talk about, much less go
about doing.

And the doing, make no mistake,
is the one thing you shouldn't
think about.

Perfect.

Life and death are perfect
because either can precede or
succeed the other. There is
nothing else in the universe
like these twins
differentiated/separated only
by our human perception, which
of course, is imperfect.

I'm great, and you?

How are you?
Now I'm really asking.
How are you?
You're standing before me now
but I've never seen you this
way before
Sit a spell.
You know I see the well behind
your 'I'm well'
Tear it down if it tears you
up.
Maybe I tease, to tease it out.
It's that I, I'm asking what I
want to be asked.
What you should ask
How am I really?

Growing pains

We, the healthy, stand in the
corridor in hushed tones and
reflected sighs.
They sit inside almost rooms
because they're almost gone.
We stand above the grave and
remain in place as they leave
this space.
We miss you. Our hearts wince.
Their pain now gone as ours
grows.

Mind the gap.

We're all a bit fractured
Bespoke fractures all our own.
Find those fractures.
Trace them with your mind and
heart.
Your search through them will
lead you to one who's whole
where you're not.
Their love will fill that
fissure.
That light will ebb and flow
and caress every deep ridge and
soft groove.
But there are parts where even
that light won't shine.
It's those gaps you mind the
most.
It's within those gaps where
your treasure can slip and be
lost forever.

Always mind that gap.

Melt

When we say goodbye, don't wait
for me to take your hand down a
sinking friendship. I'd rather
bear witness as our 'us'
bubbles into the abyss.
As the flame burns down the
stem and the sweet with the sad
blend and sink into one
another.
What's left will harden into
and round that tale we wrote
and seal one final memory.

Chute your shot

A reward.

An outfit more suited for a new
born.

A onesie for just that once.

A propeller for a ladder.

No rungs, just flight.

No stairs, just right.

Overhead, the sound of dread.

A pilot who announces that
we've reached a brand new
homestead.

Amazon Prime, not an option.

My mind transfixed only
existing in the space between
courage a trail of fear running
down my leg.

Eyes narrowing at the goggled
view of each adventurer dressed
in blue.

Silent screams all around.

Listening now for instructions
on how to avoid my own
destruction.

Out the door except there is no
floor.

My mind pressing forward into
the face of the unknown,
and through the disappearing
thought clouds that populate my
busy mind.

But this is no comic strip. In
fact, I can't even see the
fucking air strip!

Turning into AND AGAINST a
gravi-tron wind. An unnatural
smile. An unfamiliar emotion.
An object, no wings, no fuel
but ripping through the sky all
the same.

And then, suddenly something
familiar, something heavy.
Inevitable. Gravity.

I turn my dizzied gaze and
reach for that FUZZY LIME
LIFELINE, to find it isn't
there.

All at once, shock, despair.

Until my go-go gadget fingers
clasp and pull.

Gliding now, arms and legs
outstretched, my wildest dreams
and fears forever kept inside
and always in flight.

Sunrise, sunset.

Late bloomers are the only
flowers that tire out the sun.

Corporate Aid

To all my shower sirens,
driveway drummers, bedroom
bassists and office
shredders...rock on.

www.ingramcontent.com/pod-product-compliance
Lightning Source LLC
La Vergne TN
LVHW021332200726
843509LV00014B/2498